GREAT MASTERPIECES

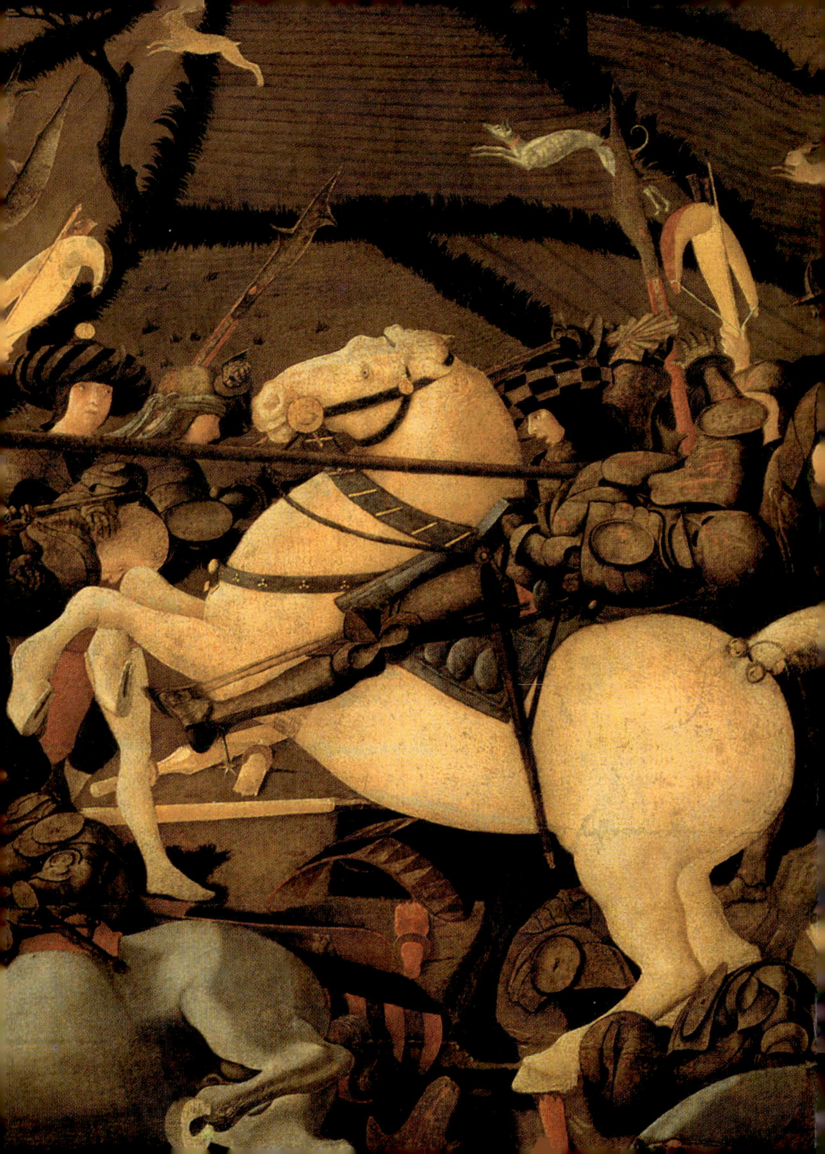

PAOLO UCCELLO

The Battle of San Romano

GIUNTI

Collection edited by Gloria Fossi
Text by: Diletta Corsini
Photographs: Rabatti-Domingie, Florence

ISBN 88-09-21470-6

It was 1st June 1432. Niccolò Mauruzi da Tolentino, captain in the service of the town of Florence during the battle against the town of Siena, reached the tower of San Romano in Valdelsa. He wanted to get a clear idea of the situation: most of the troops of the Duke of Milan, Filippo Maria Visconti, allied to the Sienese, were attacking the town of Montopoli. In a rather unusal fashion for a condottiere he corageously sought action, though the troops at his command were by far weaker. Despite being taken by suprise and attacked from both sides, the enemy reacted vigorously and almost came off better. However, in the afternoon, Florentine reinforcements were sighted under the lead of Micheletto da Cotignola. The outcome of the battle was overturned. The Duke of Milan's forces hesitated, unsure as to whether they should withdraw or inflict the final blow to Tolentino's hard pressed troops: Bernardino della Ciarda, commander who had once been close to the Florentines, but had later entered the service of the town of Siena and of the Viscontis, had to retreat with his men. Tolentino pressed on, but his soldiers, after three long hours fighting, exhausted, put an end to the pursuit allowing the Duke's forces, the *ducheschi*, to accomplish their retreat. Hence, it was an unfulfilled victory, a missed opportunity, a narrow escape, yet it was perhaps the only episode worth remembering in a battle scarce of satisfactions for the Florentines. Despite its uncertain outcome, the battle gave inspiration to one of the most important series of Italian XV century paintings: the three paintings of the *Battle of San Romano*, which Cosimo de' Medici, the Elder, commissioned from Paolo Uccello, who is described by biographer Giorgio Vasari as "the most captivating and imaginative painter to have lived since Giotto". The painting, which impresses the viewer, being the first historical subject in the gallery after a long train of religious paintings with golden backgrounds, is currently preserved in the Uffizi in Florence and depicts the central episode of the battle, the frontal clash between the troops and the ensuing repulse of Bernardino della Ciarda. The two paintings that used to hang beside it are preserved in other European galleries: in the National Gallery in London there is the painting showing Niccolò da Tolentino in the act of launching the attack, whilst in the Louvre in Paris there is the painting depicting Micheletto da Cotignola's intervention.

Where do the paintings come from? A document says that in 1492 the *Battles*, framed in gold, were part of the furniture in Lorenzo the

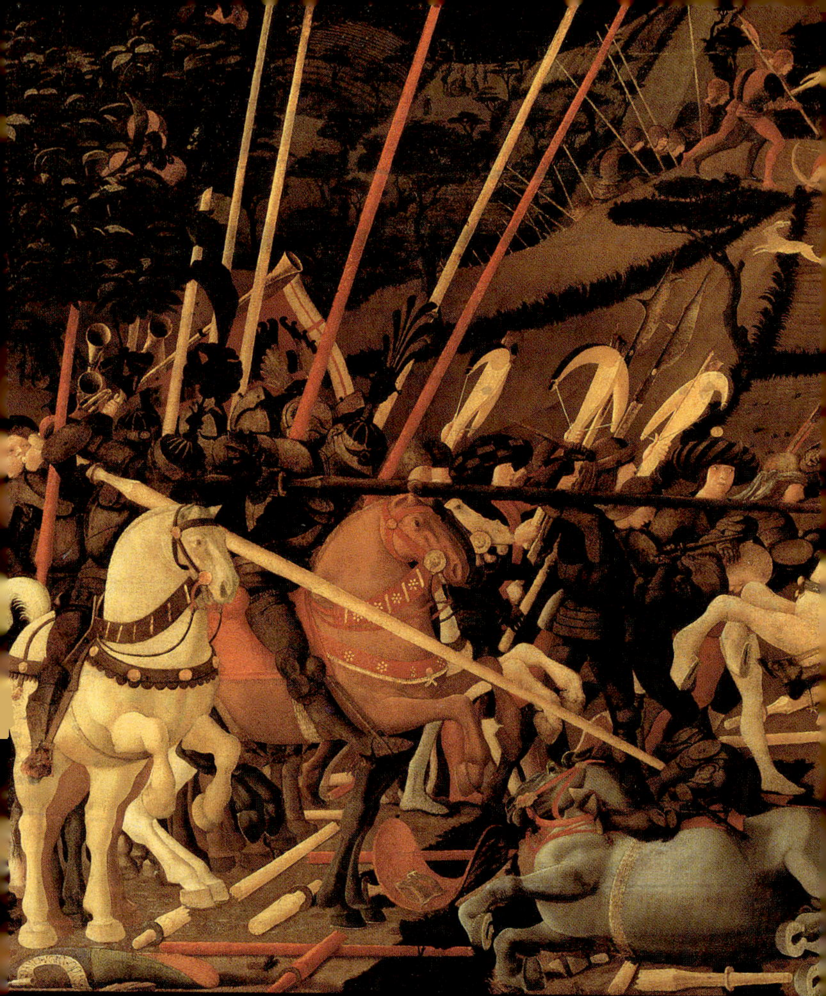

Paolo Uccello, *The Battle of San Romano*, 1435-38 circa.
Tempera on panel, 182 x 323 cm.
Florence, Uffizi Gallery, inv. 1890 no. 479.

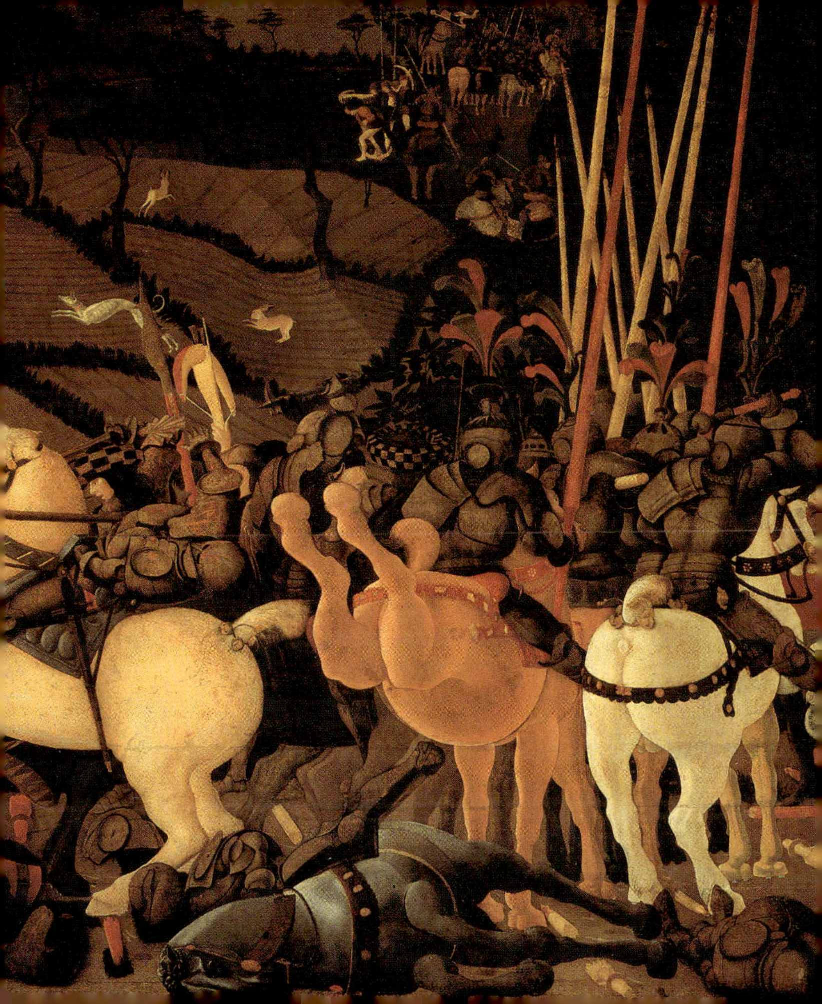

Magnificent's chamber on the ground floor of Palazzo Medici and were on show in sequence, as a monumental decoration, hanging over the high backs of the *lettucci* (the *lettuccio* was a kind of chest with a wooden back on it). This is why for a long time it was believed that the three paintings had been executed for that chamber after 1452, the year in which the Medici family, who by that time were clearly lords of Florence, moved into the new palace planned by Michelozzo. With reference to the paintings' style, this late dating hindered the assessment of Paolo Uccello's career as a painter (seemingly retracing his own steps). In addition, it obscured the reasons why Cosimo the Elder should have wanted to remember a battle so far-off and, all in all, of so little relevance for the town's destiny. And this at a time when Florence was yet re-echoing with the more decisive and overwhelming vic-

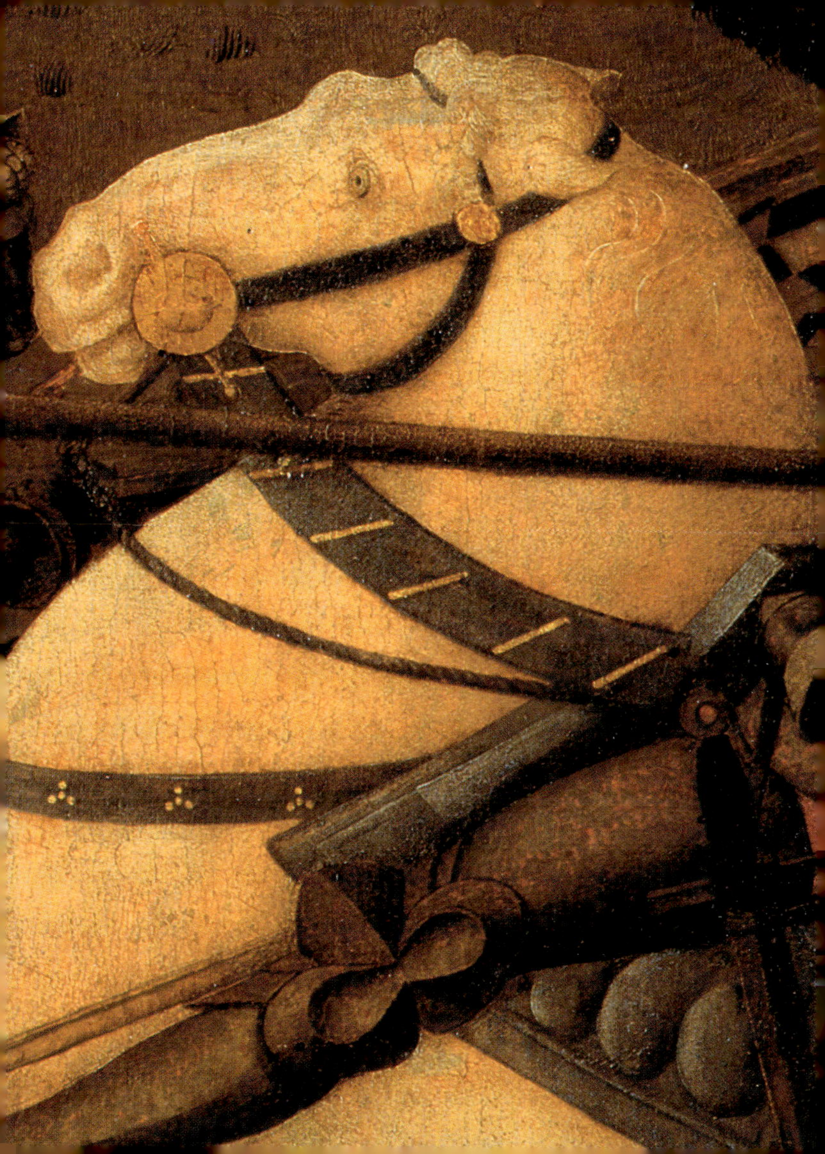

tory won at Anghiari (1440). Everything makes sense if dating is put forward to the end of the '30s in the 15th century and one considers the role the Medici family played in planning the strategy of the battle.

The Florentines were in desperate need for a victory: bankers Cosimo de' Medici and his cousin Averardo, who sought popular consensus to strengthen their political prestige, exposed themselves directly financing the endeavour and exploiting their good connections with the two captains. Cosimo managed to secure for himself the enterprising Tolentino, already a loyal friend of his (loyalty was a rare and precious quality for a condottiero); on his part, Averardo, was able to take on Cotignola, who from Spring had been encamping with his army in the area of Cascina near Pisa, awaiting for the renewal of the military contract, the *condotta*.

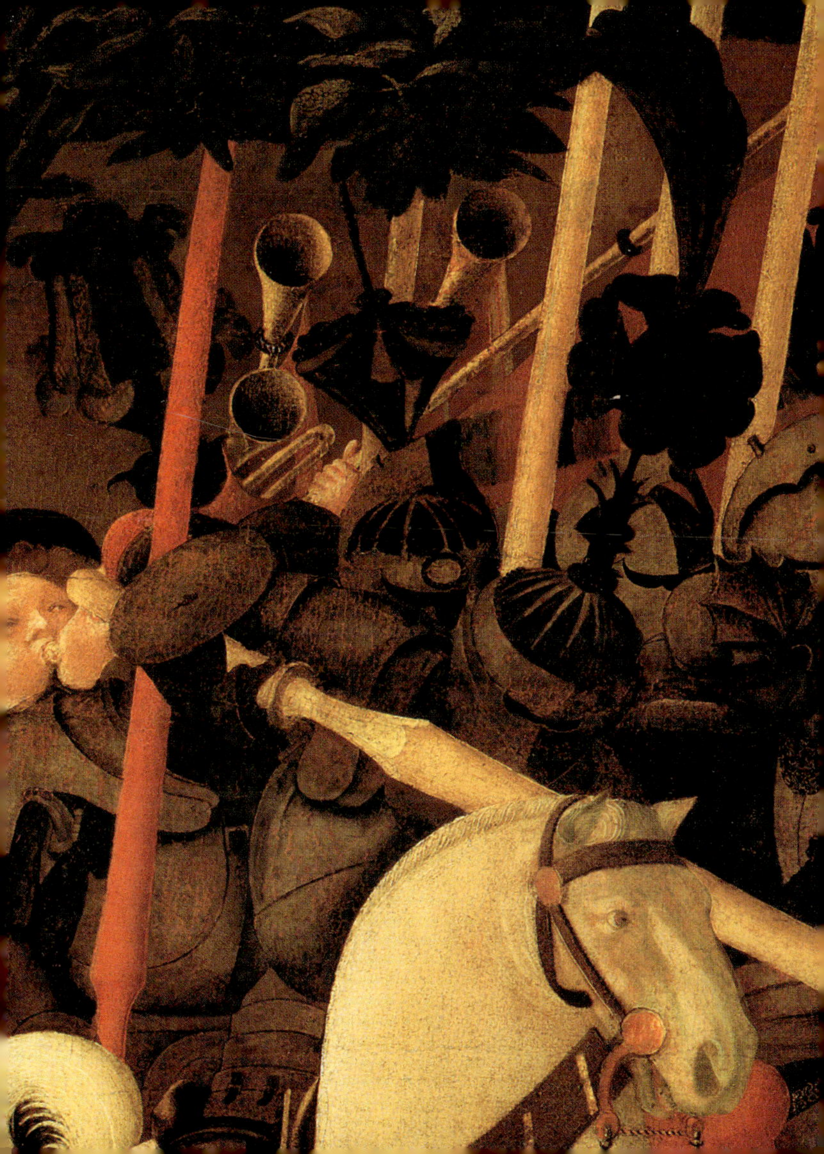

Paolo Uccello's *Battles*, which were almost certainly painted between 1435 and 1440, that is shortly after the event they depict, acquire an obvious political meaning for the Medicis, especially for Cosimo (Averardo died in 1434): through the figures of the two condottieri, the paintings celebrate the family's emergence at the leadership of Florence.

Possibly the solemn funeral decreed by the Republic in honour of Tolentino, who had been defeated in 1435 and had died prisoner in Milan, inspired Cosimo to have a pictorial cycle remembering, on the one hand, "his" *condottiero*, on the other, the family's allegiance to the town. The paintings were commissioned to Paolo Uccello before Palazzo Medici had been built. They were probably intended for a reception room in the family's old house, situated in the

 same street – Via Larga, presently Via Cavour –

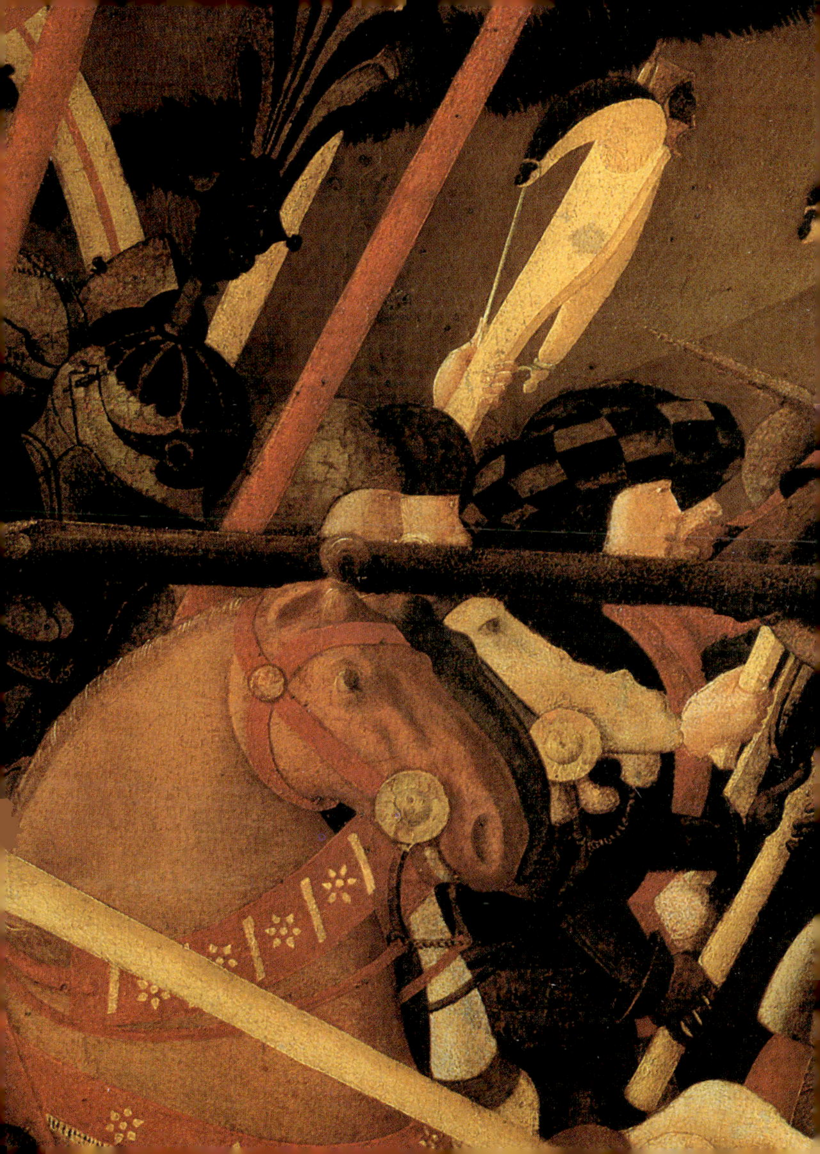

but further down, towards the basilica of San Marco. The accurate analysis of the three works has revealed cuts and alterations that have changed their original format. The paintings were originally meant to be lunettes to place-underneath the vaults of a hall. The top part was eventually cut off in order to fit the panels in Lorenzo's chamber in the new palace. The idea to re-shape the works into *tavole quadre* [square panels] probably was aimed at adapting the paintings to the dominant taste of the time, since pinnacles and lunettes were out of date in the '40s. However, it may also be that there was a political reason behind the alterations. Indeed, besides a large quantity of landscape, adjustments at this stage involved trimming out standards testifying to a display of alliances that had undergone changes. The Milanese, who in the remote history of the battle had been adversaries

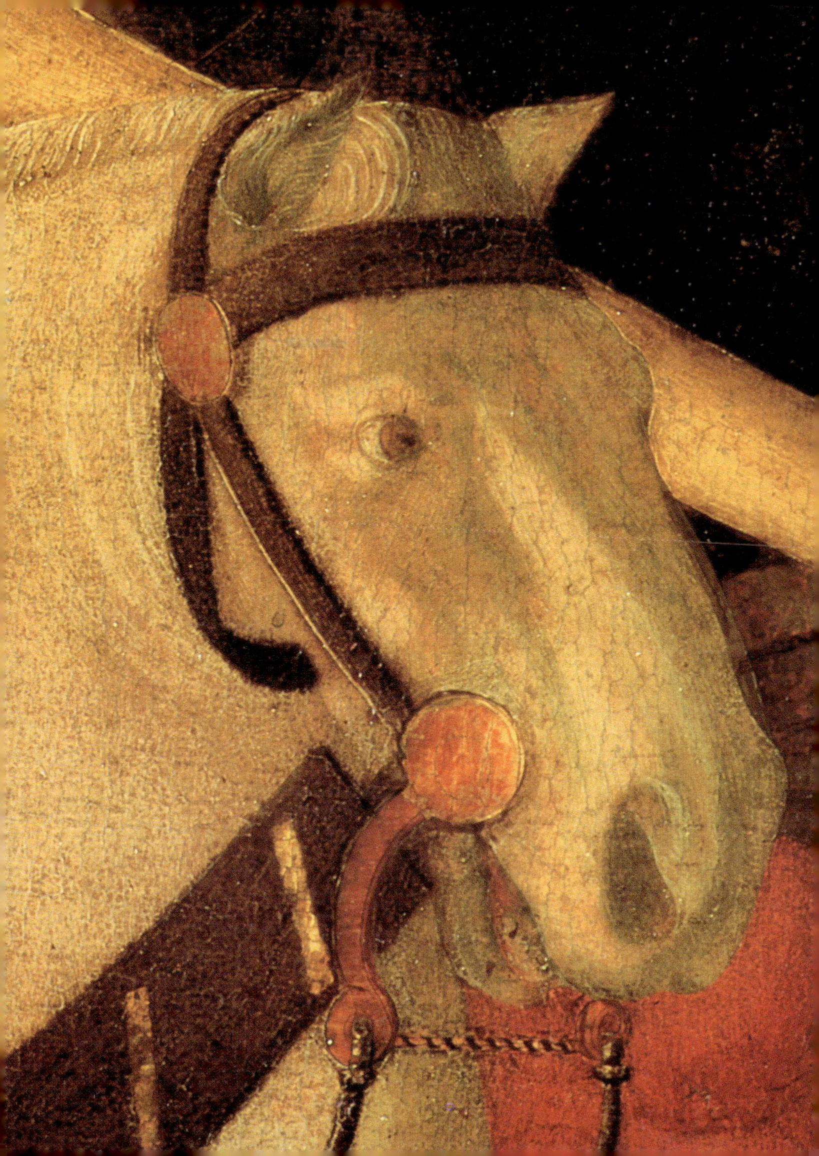

to Florence, by the time of Lorenzo the Magnificent were his allies. The old political meaning, thus masked, of the panels of *The Battle of San Romano* could easily be mixed with the numerous paintings of jousts, tournaments, hunts, "battles of dragons and lions" which made merry the magnificent abode of the lords of Florence. Another point in favour of an early dating can be obtained observing the armours. Those painted by Paolo Uccello, with round, smooth, fleeting forms, studied purposedly to avoid the enemy's blows, were in use around 1435: they are complete armours, with precise forms, entirely made in polished or burnished steel. At the beginning of the 15th century the protection of bodies still relied on hauberks (iron mail) and leather garments, or fabrics covered or lined with metal plates. Later on, in the

 second half of the century, armours underwent

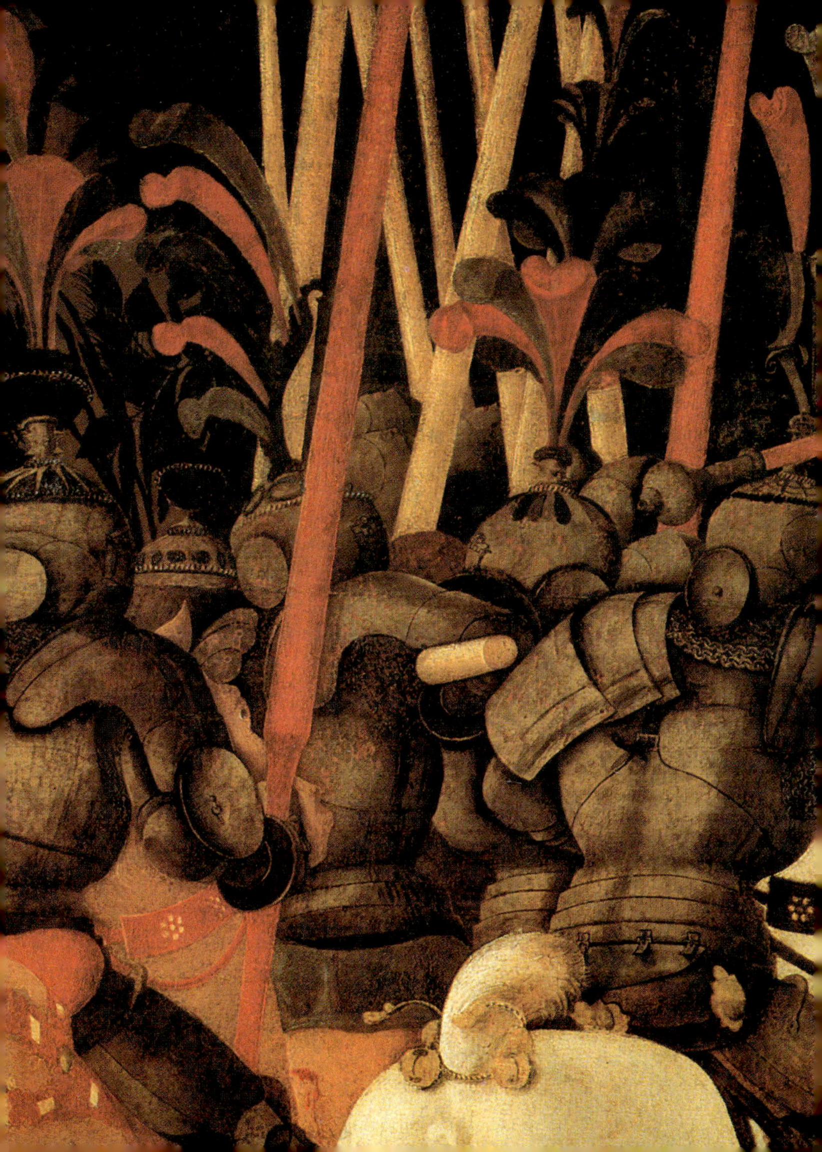

a change not in their structure but in their details, inspired by contemporary clothing.

A painter like Paolo, used to analyzing the form and the volume of things, could not help being interested in armours, which to him probably appeared as extraordinary sculptures: mobile, abstract, human-like. These splendid shining armours transformed the warriors in automata, in unusual faceless creatures who could only be recognized from their crests and the emblems shown on their shields, flags or horses' harness (in the previous century the coat of arms was always embroidered on a short tunic made of precious materials which would be worn around the knight's chest).

Paolo is said to have spent the nights immersed in his studies, and that his wife was extremely concerned with such behaviour. For the

 painter, who studied optical phenomena and

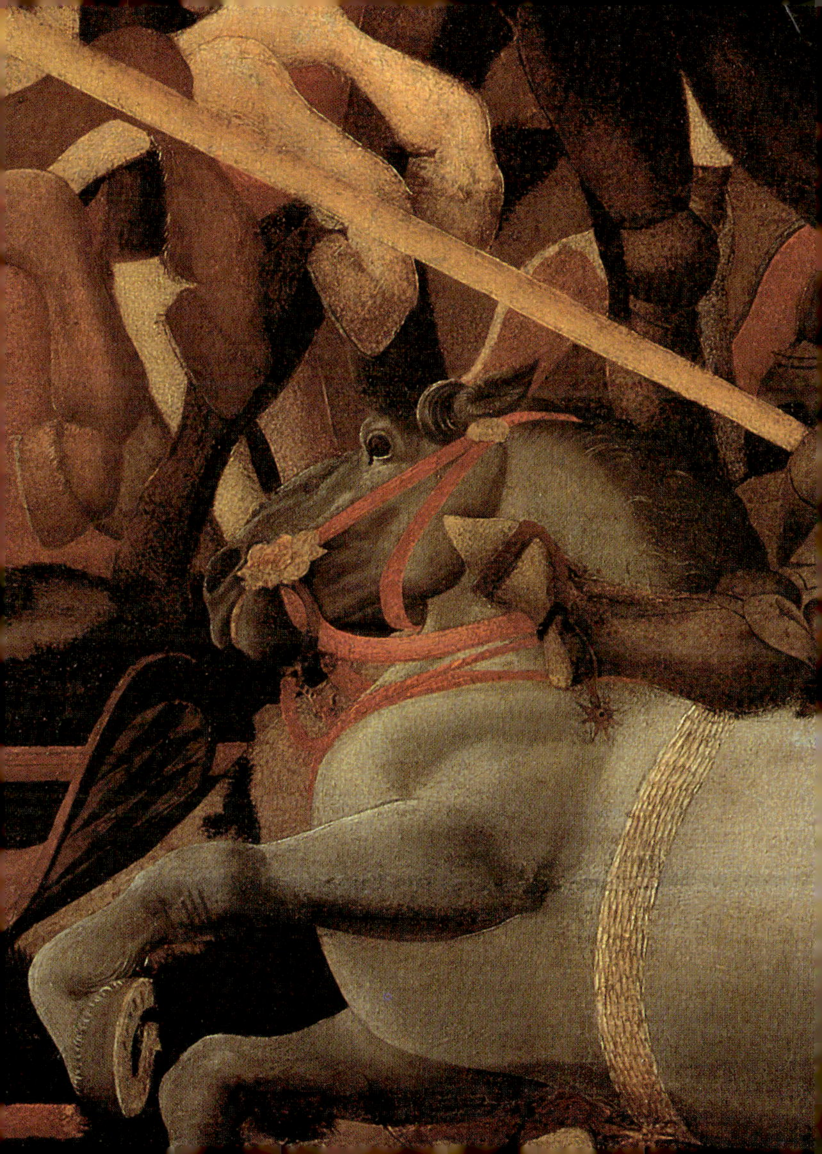

even had a "craze" for perspective, it must have been a real challenge to try and represent how distorted and multiplied images were reflected on the armours' surfaces. The armours, composed of spheres, cylinders and cones, seemed to behave like the convex and "column-like" mirrors described as early as 1270 in a treatise on perspective by the philosopher Witelo, a text that the artist knew well. To imitate the glittering of metals and the effects of translucent enamel, Paolo made use of all his painting skills, learned in Ghiberti's workshop, in Florence, and perfected during his stay in Venice (where, among other things, he dedicated himself to the difficult art of mosaic). He therefore covered armours with silver and gold leaves; subsequently, with a brush, he used to put on them a layer of "dragon's blood" – an organic resin – and rare and precious laquers. Unfortunately, old restora-

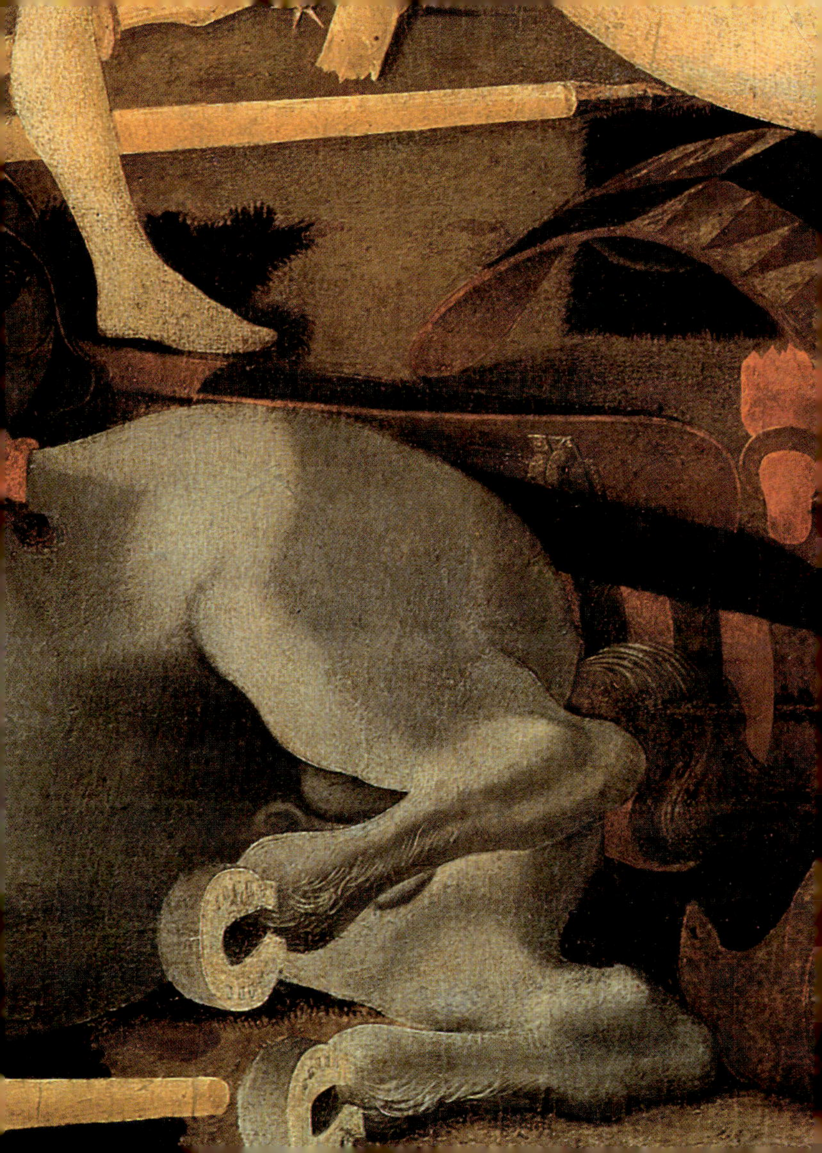

tions, meant to enhance the brilliancy of the colours, compromised the effects of this technical virtuosity. The silver leaf was in most part replaced by tinfoil, which is not as reflective. Those extraordinary layers were thus removed and the loss of the silver leaf certainly modified the matching of colours which, even though probably looked unreal in those days as well, (where on earth are orange, blue and greenish horses to be seen?), it now shows too much contrast between them, creating an unusual effect of tarsia on the flat shapes of the horses.

Surely, Paolo did not depict the battle as it really took place: there is not much blood (while the battle was far from being bloodless) and the fallen soldiers, rather than look dead, seem to be broken dummies. There is no tension, no tragic atmosphere; his representation is not realistic, but poetical. From this point of view, the Flo-

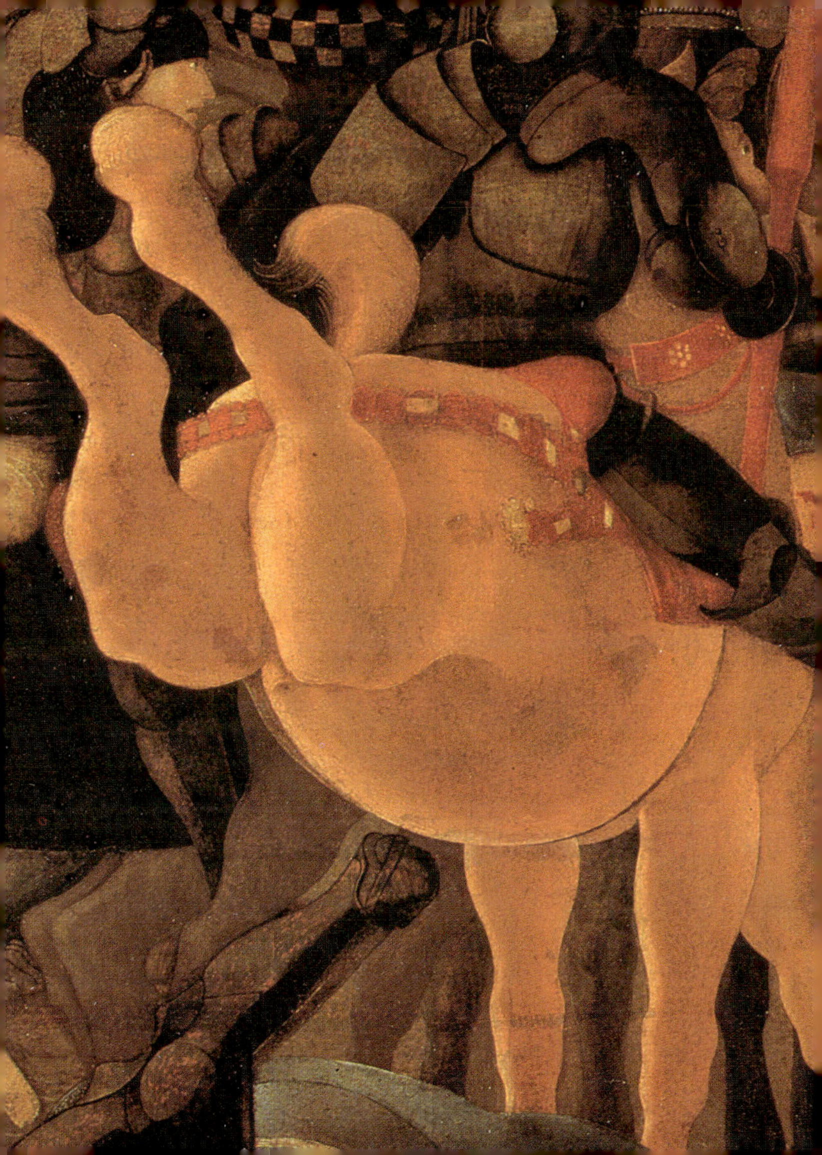

rence panel must have been the central one, because the unhorsing of Bernardino della Ciarda (an episode recorded by no historical source) well expresses the moment of victory, given by the tenaille manoeuvre of the two winning Commanders. The head of the Sienese and Visconti militia, at the centre, on a white horse, is stabbed by the long lance of an adversary and thrown off his horse; the buglers on the left, behind the crowd of lances, cross-bows and *ronconi* (weapons made of a shaft with a long convex blade provided with spikes, used by foot-soldiers), blow their instruments (the clarion) to show their joy for the victory: instead, the Sienese warriors on the right are fleeing. Their horses, incited to run, are kicking and crowding together in a space which the painting does not show. Paolo Uccello, who was in Venice when he first made use of Renaissance perspective in

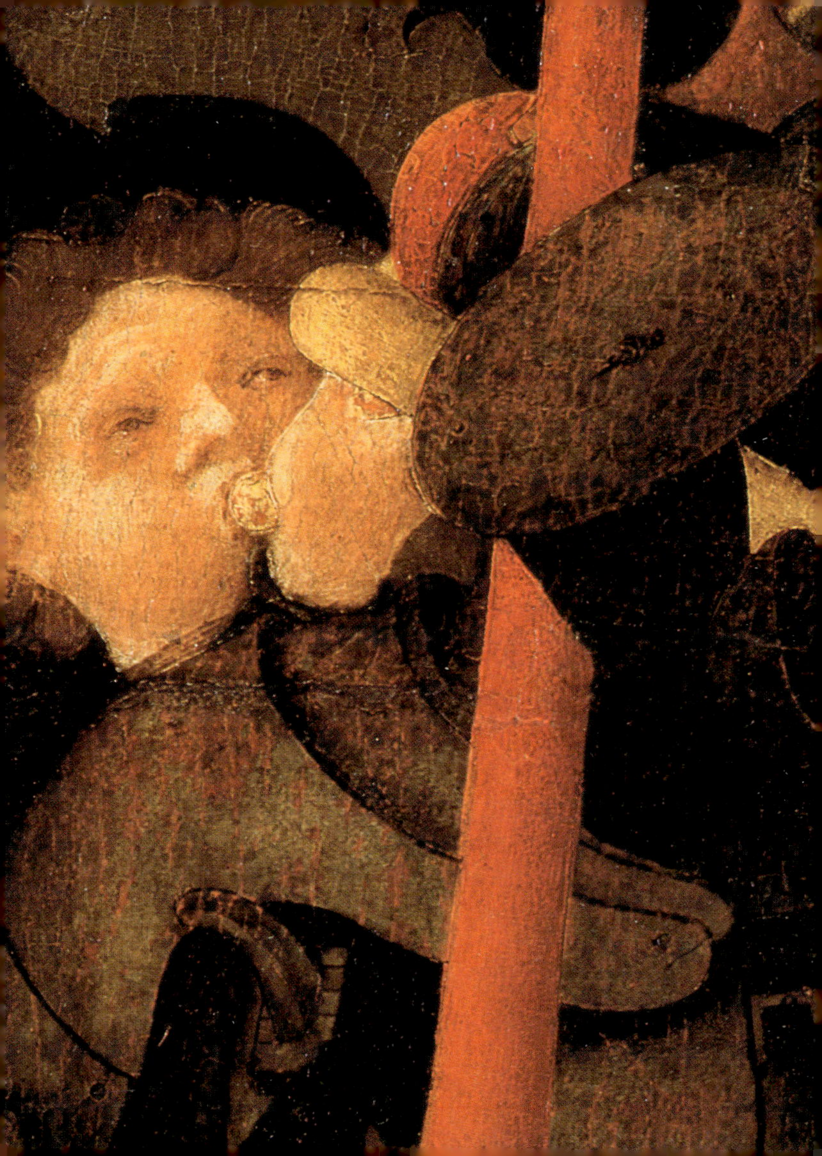

painting and sculptures, found a radical change in the artistic environment of Florence on his return home. There, the commonly accepted way of representing depth on a flat surface was by then that theorised by Brunelleschi. The alternative theories proposed by Ghiberti, which were in the forefront twenty years earlier, had difficulty in finding any followers. Paolo, who could not put up with the "straightforwardness" and consistency of Brunelleschi's perspective, continued, nonetheless, to propose several possibilities: before Uccello's paintings, the onlooker has several points of vision at his disposal. The artist's way of representing reality and distribute space does not accept the stillness of a "fixed" vision: he had a curious and restless eye, always on the move, which lingered on details, wishing to depict everything from the best point of vision. He never refused perspective, on